CULTURE IN ACTION

Vanished!

Magic Tricks and Great Escapes

Sean Stewart Price

Raintree

www.raintreepublishers.co.uk
Visit our website to find out more information about Raintree books.

To order:
Phone 0845 6044371
Fax +44 (0) 1865 312263
Email myorders@raintreepublishers.co.uk

Customers from outside the UK please telephone +44 1865 312262

Raintree is an imprint of Capstone Global Library Limited, a company incorporated in England and Wales having its registered office at 7 Pilgrim Street, London, EC4V 6LB – Registered company number: 6695582

First published in hardback in 2011

Edited by Louise Galpine, Megan Cotugno, and Abby Colich
Designed by Ryan Frieson
Original illustrations © Capstone Global Library Ltd
Illustrated by Cavedweller Studio, Randy Schirz
Picture research by Liz Alexander
Originated by Capstone Global Library Ltd
Printed in China by China Translation & Printing Services Ltd

ISBN 978 1 40621 697 4
15 14 13 12 11 10
10 9 8 7 6 5 4 3 2 1

British Library Cataloguing in Publication Data
Price, Sean Stewart
Vanished!: Magic tricks and great escapes. – (Culture in action)
793.8-dc22

A full catalogue record for this book is available from the British Library.

Acknowledgements
We would like to thank the following for permission to reproduce photographs: © Capstone Publishers p. **5** (Karon Dubke); © Masterfile p. **18**; Alamy pp. **4** (© VirtualSilver), **12**, **13**, **15** (© The Protected Art Archive), **24** (© Travel India), **27** (© Radius Images), **28** (© Richard Levine), **29** (© Findlay); Corbis pp. **7** (© Bettmann), **10** (© Andrew Brusso), **20** (© Scott Harrison/ Retna Ltd.), **25** (© John Lund/ Blend Images); Getty Images pp. **8** (The Bridgeman Art Library), **9** (Tooga/Stone), **14** (Hulton Archive), **16** (Ethan Miller), **17** (WireImage/Don Arnold), **22** (AFP/Valery Hache); Science Photo Library p. **11**; The Bridgeman Art Library International p. **6** (Brooklyn Museum of Art, New York, USA/Charles Edwin Wilbour Fund.

Cover photograph of George, The Supreme Master of Magic poster, 1928 reproduced with permission of Corbis (© Swim Ink 2, LLC).

We would like to thank David Goodsell and Jackie Murphy for their invaluable help in the preparation of this book.

Author
Sean Stewart Price is the author of more than 40 books for young people and teachers, on subjects ranging from history and science to public health.

Literacy consultant
Jackie Murphy is Director of Arts at a centre of teaching and learning. She works with teachers, artists, and school leaders internationally.

Expert
David R. Goodsell is a past national president of the Society of American Magicians and holds a Member of the Inner Magic Circle with Gold Star degree in The Magic Circle (London). He has received many awards, fellowships, and Honorary memberships, and has been a lifelong educator.

Contents

The world of magic 4

The first magicians 6

Famous magicians 10

Modern magic 16

Magic and make-believe 20

Tricky stuff 24

The secret to magic 28

Glossary 30

Find out more 31

Index 32

Get permission – it works magic

Like the thumb illusion, most magic tricks are harmless. But some can be dangerous. Make sure you get a parent's or guardian's permission before trying any magic.

Some words are printed in bold, **like this**. You can find out what they mean by looking in the glossary on page 30.

The world of magic

The word *magic* can mean different things. Some people talk about magic when they mean special powers, like **witchcraft** or **sorcery**. They believe that some people can fly on broomsticks or turn a cup into a cat.

But there is another type of magic. That is the magic of fooling people. Magicians are performers who practise this type of magic. They make it look as though they can fly on a broomstick or turn a cup into a cat. But they are really doing tricks. We say magicians create **illusions**, or actions that look real but are not.

The magic word: *abracadabra*

The word *abracadabra* gets a lot of use in modern magic shows. It comes from the ancient Romans. They believed saying the word could cure people of fevers. Today, magicians use *abracadabra* like they are casting a spell. For example, they say it just as they make a scarf disappear or water spurt from their wand.

When magicians do tricks, they are actually creating illusions.

The separated thumb trick

This book is about the magic of tricks. Almost everybody can do one. Think about the separated thumb trick. Bend both of your thumbs at the knuckle. Place the knuckle of your right thumb next to the knuckle of the left thumb, so that it is facing the same direction as the fingers on your left hand. Take your right forefinger and cover the place where your knuckles meet. Move your right hand back and forth. This makes it look as though you have removed the end of your left thumb!

Welcome to the world of illusion and magic!

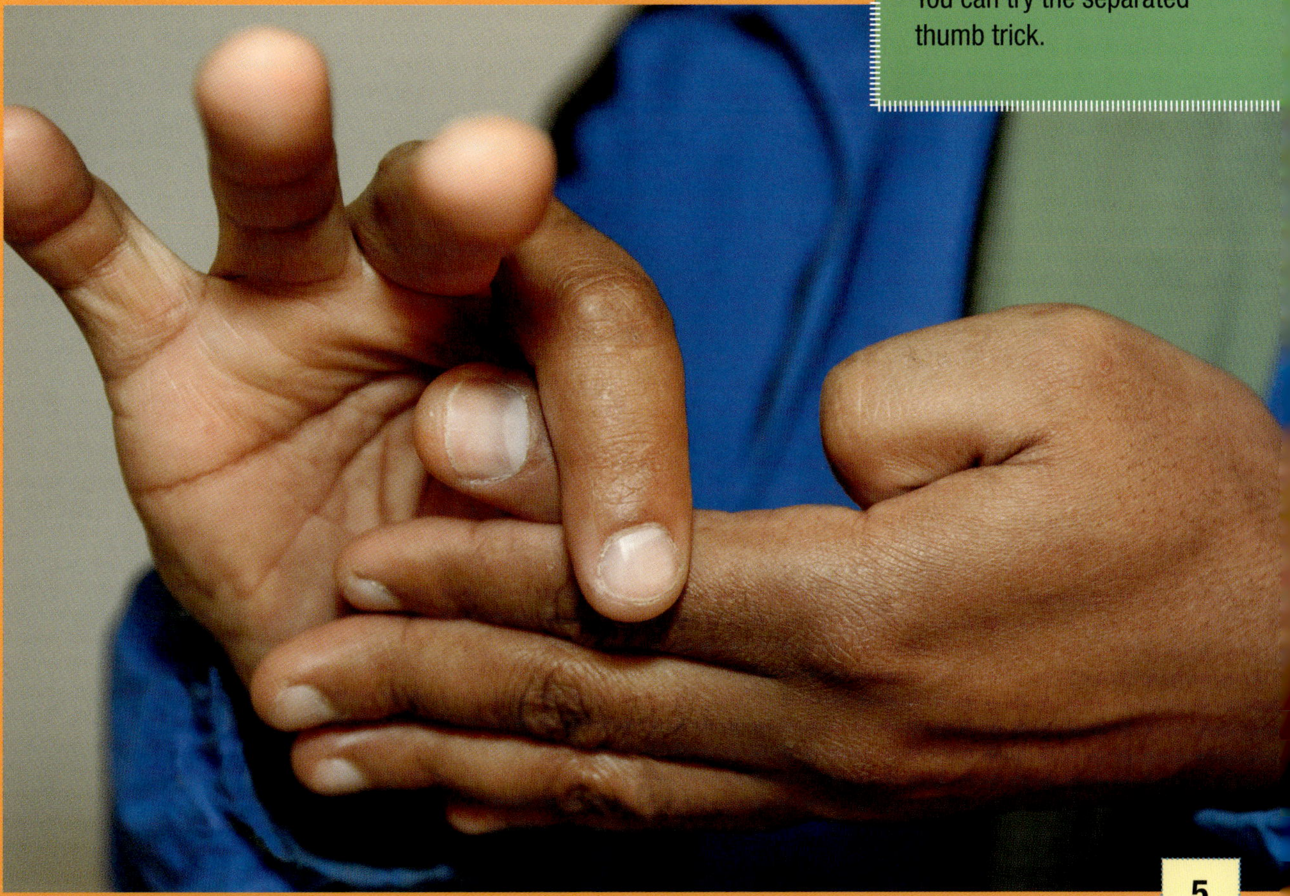

You can try the separated thumb trick.

The first magicians

Magic tricks have been with us since ancient times. The earliest known magician was an ancient Egyptian called Dedi. One day Dedi was called before the pharaoh (ruler) Cheops. Cheops was the leader who built Egypt's largest pyramid. He ruled Egypt from about 2589 to 2566 BC.

For his first trick, Dedi cut the head off a goose. Then he reattached the head and – behold – the animal was alive again. Dedi repeated this trick with a pelican and an ox. But he refused Cheops' request to try it on a man. Dedi also made a lion obey him.

The ancient Egyptian Dedi performed magic for Pharaoh Cheops (also known as Khufu), seen here.

Biblical magic tricks

Some people use magic tricks to make it look as though they have special powers. This happened in the **Bible**. The Hebrew leader Daniel lived under Cyrus the Great, the king of Persia. Cyrus believed in the god Bel. Each day Cyrus sent food and wine to Bel's temple. Each day the food and wine were sealed inside the temple. By the next day, it had all disappeared.

Cyrus the Great ruled Persia in the 500s BC.

Cyrus believed the god Bel must be taking the food. But Daniel scattered ashes on the temple floor before it was sealed one night. The next day footprints could be seen in the ashes. The footprints led to a secret chamber. This showed that Bel's priests had really taken the food and wine. Cyrus had all the priests killed. The temple was destroyed.

The magician king

Around 135 BC a Roman slave in Sicily called Eunus used magic tricks to start a slave **revolt**. Eunus could breathe fire and make things disappear. People thought he was some kind of **sorcerer** and decided to follow him. The revolt was briefly successful, and he became a king. But he was not in power for long and was eventually killed.

This engraving shows people believed to be witches being burned in 1555.

Magic in the Middle Ages

Being a magician during the Middle Ages could be dangerous. The Middle Ages lasted from about AD 500 to 1500 in Europe. During that time, the Christian church saw magic as **witchcraft**. Church officials believed witches received help from devils or demons.

Magicians who did tricks could be punished. In the 1400s, one girl in Cologne, Germany, got in trouble for her magic show. She ripped a handkerchief apart and then made it whole again. It is a simple magic trick that magicians have done for centuries. But church leaders put her on trial (sent her to court) for witchcraft.

Performing for kings and queens

Despite these problems, many kings and queens still liked magicians. In the late 1500s, the favourite magician of European royalty was an Italian called Girolamo Scotto. Scotto did amazing card tricks. He might ask a person to think of a card. Then Scotto could pull that card from the deck. When one person said he or she thought of "nothing", Scotto pulled out a blank card.

Scotto was a diplomat. That means he represented his country overseas. He never performed for the public. Instead he used his magic only before powerful people. One queen offered him a small fortune to see how he did his tricks. But not everyone was charmed. In 1601 King James VI of Scotland wrote that Scotto could only get his power from the devil.

The magic word: *Topit*

A **Topit** is a large secret pocket in a magician's jacket or trousers. It allows him or her to store items to be used in tricks. Pickpockets also use Topits. They store wallets and objects they have stolen in there.

Magicians use Topits to hide the objects that they make disappear.

Famous magicians

Jacob Philadelphia became the first great magician in the United States. He was a plump man whose real name was Jacob Meyer. He used the name of his hometown as his stage name.

Philadelphia travelled throughout Europe. He performed before kings, queens, and other royalty. They saw him do fancy card tricks. But people really gasped at the ghostly figures he created. Philadelphia used smoke and a light projector to create these **illusions**. He also used what looked like an ordinary pen made out of a bird's feather. But it could write in several different colours.

The magic word: *cover*

A **cover** is something used to conceal a trick while it is being done. For example, a magician waves a handkerchief over his hand while flowers appear. The handkerchief is a cover.

A handkerchief is an example of a cover. It is used to conceal something while a magician is carrying out a trick.

VISUAL ACTIVITY

Fooling the eye

Magicians like to say "the hand is quicker than the eye". That is not true. But the eye can be fooled. Look over the following shapes. See if you can tell how they fool the eye.

1. Necker Cube
   Look at this cube for a few seconds. Try to decide which corner is nearest to you. The answer will switch as you keep looking. That is because your brain cannot decide what it is looking at. You can control this switching back and forth somewhat. But after a while, your mind will do it on its own.

2. Hermann Grid
   Look at one of the black squares. You will probably see grey spots where the white bars cross. But those spots are not there. Your mind is making it appear as though they are there. Why? Because to your mind, those areas are less white than the rest of the white bars.

Now take one of these tricks and show it to other people. Explain only what you need to without giving away the illusion. Closely watch their reactions. Discuss it with them. Did they react the way you did?

Herrmann the Great

We often think of magicians as wearing a black jacket with a top hat. That tradition started with magicians in the 1800s. Perhaps the most famous of these magicians was Frenchman Alexander Herrmann.

Magician Herrmann the Great became a master of sleight of hand.

Sleight of hand

Herrmann the Great, as he was called, came from a family of magicians. He became a master of **sleight of hand**, or **prestidigitation**. It means using quick fingers to fool the eye. Experienced magicians must often work for years to become fast enough to perform before an audience.

Herrmann enjoyed dazzling people on and off the stage. Once he **produced** cigars from the beard of US President Ulysses S. Grant. If he had to pay for something, Herrmann seemed to grab the money out of the air. He made glasses vanish and reappear when eating with friends.

Grand illusions

On stage Herrmann also did grand illusions. In one trick, his wife and assistant, Adelaide, seemed to be burned alive. Then she magically reappeared. In another, Herrmann caught the bullets shot at him by a firing squad. This was dangerous, as the bullets were real.

The Queen of Magic

Herrmann the Great died in 1896 at the age of 52. His sudden death left his widow, Adelaide, with very little money. Fortunately, she was an experienced magician as well. Adelaide spent the next 31 years touring the United States and Europe. She used many of the same illusions done by her husband. She could turn a water canister into flags or produce a cage full of doves out of nowhere. People called her the "Queen of Magic".

This poster advertises an Adelaide Herrmann magic show.

Houdini

When Ehrich Weiss was a young boy, his family moved from Hungary to the United States. Originally Weiss worked for a locksmith. He learned all there was to know about breaking locks. His hero was a famous French magician called Jean-Eugène Robert-Houdin. Weiss renamed himself "Houdini" in Houdin's honour and became a magician himself.

Houdini quickly became known as the "Handcuff King". He could escape from any set of handcuffs. But that was not all. He also escaped from a straitjacket. That was a heavy canvas coat used to control mentally disturbed people.

In this photo, Houdini hangs from a crane and tries to escape out of a straitjacket.

Escape artist

Houdini moved on to even more daring escapes. Police would strip him naked and then put on 10 pairs of handcuffs and leg irons. Houdini escaped every one. Police then put him in supposedly "escape-proof" jail cells. Houdini quickly freed himself.

Perhaps his most daring escape was the "Chinese Water Torture Cell". Houdini was lowered into a locked tank full of water. He had to escape before he drowned. Houdini always made it out in two minutes.

Houdini died suddenly in 1926. Even today, he remains the most famous magician of all time. Sometimes people call a daring escape "pulling a Houdini".

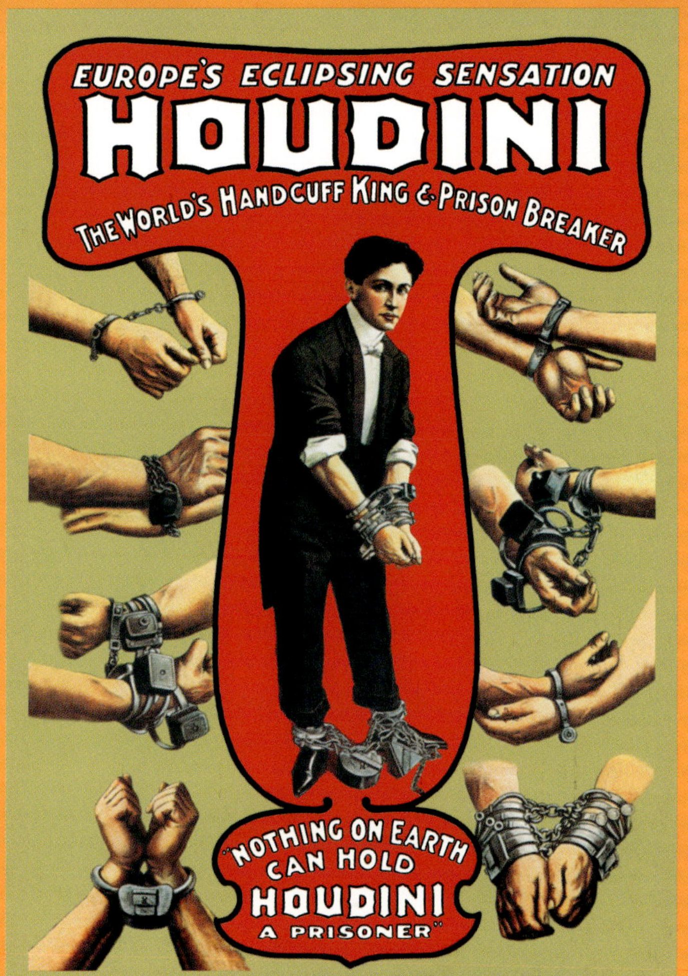

This poster from 1906 advertises Houdini as the "Handcuff King".

Houdini and the mediums

In Houdini's day, people called **mediums** claimed to be in contact with the dead. They would make it seem as though bells rang or trumpets blew from across the room. Houdini knew they were using magic tricks. He became angry that mediums were using magic to claim that they had special powers. He spent a lot of time proving that mediums were fakes.

Modern magic

Most magic shows today are just like old-fashioned ones. A magician and an assistant do clever tricks. The magician might baffle people by making coins disappear or a rabbit come out of a hat.

Magician Hans Klok is a featured act in a hotel in Las Vegas, USA.

But modern magic shows can also be **spectacles**. Some of the biggest magic shows can be found in Las Vegas, USA. These shows feature all kinds of **special effects**. Special lighting helps magicians hide or reveal certain tricks. The same is true of fog and smoke machines. Lasers help wow the audience. They also distract the audience from things the magician wants to hide.

In on the trick

Modern magic shows can be held almost anywhere. The US magician David Copperfield once made an entire airliner disappear. A ring of audience members circled the plane. It was then surround by a giant canvas. A television audience watched the plane disappear.

But the television audience did not know something. Some of the audience members were in on the trick. As the canvas hid the plane, these people stepped aside and let the plane be towed way. Then the canvas was pulled away and – as if by magic – the plane was gone!

Quick hands, quick thinking

In 2006 a robber in Florida, USA, threatened David Copperfield with a gun and demanded his money. Copperfield used **sleight of hand** to make the robber think he had nothing in his pockets. In fact, he had a wallet and a mobile phone. Once the robber left, Copperfield called the police. They quickly caught the robber.

Magician David Copperfield travels all over the world to perform magic shows.

Magicians' assistants must be just as skilled as the magician.

Magician assistants

Some people are magicians' assistants. These assistants are the ones who are sawed in half or floated off the ground. Many people do not realise that these assistants have to be just as skilled as the magicians themselves. One false move can blow the magician's **illusion**.

Sawed in half

Take the trick of sawing an assistant in half. There are many ways to do this illusion. In one of them, an assistant tucks herself up in the box where her head is. Meanwhile, pretend feet moved by a machine – or another assistant's legs – kick out of the other box. The boxes are separated. To the audience, it appears as if the assistant has been cut in half.

During this trick, the assistant in the box has to move and act naturally. She cannot appear to be curled up in a small box. And when she comes out, she must look as though she was lying down, not all curled up.

Women magicians

Magicians have traditionally been men. In recent years, more women have begun to perform as magicians in their own right. For example, US magician Jinger Leigh works with a partner, magician Mark Kalin. Together they run a magic theatre in Reno, USA, called the Magic Underground. The Chinese magician Magic Jade works alone.

The magic words: *apparatus* and *gimmick*

An **apparatus** is an object the audience sees that is used to create a trick. A box in which a magician's assistant disappears is an apparatus.

A **gimmick** is something the audience does not see that helps with a trick. A magnet that makes a coin disappear would be a gimmick.

Magic and make-believe

People love stories about make-believe. Wizards in books and films such as Harry Potter can make almost anything happen. It is fun to think about having that kind of power. Who wouldn't want to make a potion that gives you good luck? Who wouldn't want to fly on a broomstick?

Some people still confuse this made-up magic with real magic tricks. In fact, some magicians have encouraged this belief. Posters for magic shows sometimes still show a devil, angel, ghost, or some other **supernatural** figure guiding a magician. The US magician Criss Angel gives his shows names like "Supernatural". This touches on the old belief that magicians need help to create such amazing displays. It also makes people more curious about the magic show.

But like most magicians, Angel makes it clear that he has no special powers. Similarly, Houdini once said that the only special powers magicians have are hard work and skill.

Some magicians, such as Criss Angel, encourage belief in the supernatural.

MUSIC ACTIVITY

How to make sound effects

Modern magicians often rely on sound effects. These sound effects make their performances more dramatic. Making some sound effects is surprisingly simple. You will need a microphone and the items listed with each sound effect. Experiment!

Steps to follow:

1. Create sound effects. Here are some ideas:

   Voice on a telephone: Speak into a plastic cup.

   Thunder: Shake a flexible baking tray or some other thin piece of metal.

   Rain: Put some dried peas in a metal pie pan. Then move the peas around in a circular motion.

   Fire: Crumple up a large piece of cellophane.

   Bird flying: Flap a leather glove.

   Wind: Pull a piece of silk or polyester cloth across a cloth chair.

   Gunshot: Hit a ruler on a flat wooden surface such as a desk.

2. Put some of the sound effects together, such as fire and wind, or thunder and rain. See if you can make them sound as real as possible while you record them.

Play around with different objects to see what sound effects you can create.

3. Create a magical moment. Try to use the sound effects with a magic trick you have read about in this book. Or use them to act out a scene from a favourite book or film in front of your friends or family.

Magician Uri Geller wants people to believe that he can bend spoons with his mind. Do you think this is true?

Pulling a fast one

Honest magicians tell people that they do not have special powers. They cannot actually make someone disappear. They cannot actually float off the ground. When they do these things, it is a trick.

Most people know this. But they still like to see magic shows. They understand that the magician's job is to fool them. The mystery is in how they do it. That keeps people watching. They want to find out how the tricks work.

Some people use magic tricks to claim that they have special powers. One of the best-known examples is Israeli-British magician Uri Geller. In the 1970s, Geller became internationally famous. He said that he could use the power of his mind to bend spoons and other metal objects. He also said that he could describe hidden drawings and make watches stop or run faster.

Many magicians laughed at Geller's claims. Everything Geller did can be done by any magician (see page 23).

PERFORMANCE ACTIVITY

How to magically bend spoons

Steps to follow:

1. Find a metal spoon that is okay to ruin.
2. Now prepare the spoon. Gently bend the neck of the spoon back and forth. You want to weaken the metal, not break it.
3. Straighten the spoon so that it looks normal.
4. Then put your finger and thumb over the weakened area. Gently rub it for several seconds.
5. As you rub, begin putting pressure so that it slowly bends.
6. Take your performance to an audience. When you do the trick, tell the audience that you are focusing all your mental power on bending the spoon. Make the audience believe this. Make it look like you are focusing hard – even draining yourself of energy. You can even use the word *abracadabra!*

Concentrate hard to make people believe that you are bending a spoon with your mind.

Tricky stuff

The following are a few of the major categories of magic tricks.

Magician Jadugar Akash practises the art of escape.

Producing

In **producing**, an object suddenly appears. The best-known example of this is pulling a rabbit out of a hat.

Vanishing

Vanishing occurs when an object suddenly disappears. For example, a magician locks his assistant in a cabinet, taps his wand, and – presto! – his assistant has disappeared.

Transforming

In **transforming**, once again the magician locks an assistant in a cabinet. But this time, the magician and assistant trade places in the blink of an eye.

Penetrating

In **penetrating**, one object seems to move through another. Magicians often link metal rings together, or ropes appear to pass through a body.

Escaping

The magician is locked up and then escapes. Usually this is done behind a **cover**. The cover hides a **gimmick** that sets the magician free.

Levitating

In most **levitating** tricks, the magician seems to cause an assistant to rise and be suspended in the air. A strong bar sticks out from a curtain. The assistant rests on a small platform or pole attached to that bar.

This magician is making it look like this woman is levitating.

Restoring

Magicians make it appear as though they can **restore** a card that has been burned or a rope that is cut in two. This trick usually works one of two ways. Either the object was destroyed and secretly replaced, or the object only appeared to be destroyed.

Mentalism

In **mentalism** a magician seems to read someone's mind. Sometimes the magician just makes guesses based on the appearance of the audience member. Sometimes secret assistants spy on audience members before the performance. They then relay information to the magician.

Rules for magicians

Magic is a special kind of performance that goes back centuries. Throughout time, magicians have learned important things about putting on a good show.

Never repeat a trick for the same audience

Once you have done a trick, the audience knows what to look for. If you repeat the trick, some people might be able to tell how you did it. Then the **illusion** is blown.

People in the audience may ask you to repeat a trick. Always be ready with another, better trick to distract them.

Never reveal how you did a trick

People like magic because of its mystery. Take away the mystery, and they will not be interested any more. If people ask you to reveal a trick, tell them that a good magician never gives away secrets. And if they still demand it, tell them to look in a magic book at the library.

Control the stage

Most magic tricks work if the audience is in front of the magician. People to the side or behind the magician might be able to see how the trick works. Make sure that the audience is in a place that works for your tricks.

This boy is performing a trick for his audience.

Remember the audience

Doing magic tricks can be hard. A magician on the stage has a lot on his or her mind. The magician must think about the details of a trick. They must also look ahead to the next trick. It can be easy to forget about entertaining the audience, but that is an essential part of being a good magician.

The secret to magic

What is the best way to become a magician? You must practise, practise, practise. Work on a trick over and over again. It should become automatic to you. Your hands and the rest of your body should simply know what to do.

Remember that it is easy to give away the secret of a trick. The wrong body movement or glance can signal what is about to happen. For instance, do not squint just as a trick is about to be revealed. If you do, it will look as though you are working too hard. The trick should appear effortless. As you do this, look into the eyes of your audience members. They should be paying close attention.

This magician is performing a magic trick for children. Children can learn about magic by watching others do magic tricks.

Magicians must practise their patter in order to keep their audiences entertained.

Good patter

Also work on your **patter**. Patter is the talking magicians do while they perform. Good patter can turn ordinary tricks into a great performance. Dull patter can make even exciting tricks look boring.

When you practise, record your patter. Make sure that you have chosen the right words for each trick. Also make sure that your tone and volume are correct. You want your voice to sound dramatic at just the right moments.

Patter can be hard to do sometimes. The best idea is to watch other magicians. Also rent DVDs and watch television programmes about magic (see page 31). They will give you clues about good patter. Many magicians like to tell jokes. Make sure that your jokes are funny before you work them into your act.

Relax and enjoy

Make sure you sound confiden and make it clear that you are having fun. That will put your audience at ease. People will want to watch you perform.

Glossary

apparatus object the audience sees that is used to create a trick

Bible religious texts used by Christians

cover something a magician uses to conceal an object before revealing an illusion

gimmick device the audience does not see that helps a magician perform an illusion

illusion action that looks real but is not

levitating type of magic in which something rises and appears to float in mid-air

medium someone who claims to be able to speak with the dead

mentalism type of magic in which the magician appears to read minds

patter the talking that magicians do when they perform

penetrating type of magic in which one solid object seems to move through another

prestidigitation type of magic that means it is quick enough to fool the human eye

producing type of magic in which an object suddenly appears, like pulling a rabbit out of a hat

restoring type of magic in which an object that has been destroyed appears to be restored to its original condition

revolt fight back against something

sleight of hand type of magic in which the illusion is caused by the skill of the magician's hands

sorcerer someone who has special supernatural powers over objects and other people. This is another word for *witch* or *wizard*.

sorcery use of special supernatural powers over objects and other people

special effect trick that makes something imaginary seem real

spectacle unusual and dramatic event or display

supernatural something outside of what can be seen with the natural eye or what can be proven to exist

Topit large secret pocket in magician's clothing for storing objects used in tricks

transforming type of magic in which two objects suddenly switch places

vanishing type of magic in which an object suddenly disappears

witchcraft having special powers over people and objects, such as the power to fly on broomsticks

Find out more

Books

The Complete Idiot's Guide to Street Magic, Tom Ogden (Alpha Books, 2007)

Harry Houdini: A Magical Life, Elizabeth MacLeod (Kids Can Press, 2005)

The Magic Handbook series, Joe Fullman (QED Publishing, 2008)

Magic Tricks to Make and Do, Ben Denne (Usborne Publishing, 2008)

DVD

A Beginner's Guide to Magic Tricks (IMC Vision, 2007)

Website

The Young Magicians Club
www.theyoungmagiciansclub.co.uk
This website provides information about the Young Magicians Club.

Index

"abracadabra" 4, 23
Angel, Criss 20
apparatus 19
assistants 13, 16, 18, 19, 24, 25
audiences 12, 16, 17, 19, 23, 25, 26, 27, 28, 29

Bible 7

card tricks 9, 10, 25
Cheops 6
"Chinese Water Torture Cell" 15
Copperfield, David 17
cover 10, 24
Cyrus the Great 7

Daniel 7
Dedi 6

Egypt 6
escape tricks 14, 15, 24
Eunus 7

Geller, Uri 22
gimmicks 19, 24
Grant, Ulysses S. 12

Herrmann, Adelaide 13
Herrmann the Great 12, 13
Houdini 14, 15, 20

James VI, king of Scotland 9
jokes 29

Kalin, Mark 19

Las Vegas, USA 16
Leigh, Jinger 19
levitation tricks 18, 22, 25

Magic Jade 19
Magic Underground theatre 19
mediums 15
mentalism tricks 25
Middle Ages 8

patter 29
penetrating tricks 24
Persia 7
Philadelphia, Jacob 10
practice 28, 29
producing tricks 12, 13, 24

repetition 26
restoration tricks 25
Robert-Houdin, Jean-Eugène 14
Rome 4, 7
rules 26

"sawed in half" trick 18, 19
Scotto, Girolamo 9
secrets 7, 9, 25, 26, 28
"separated thumb" trick 5
sleight of hand 12, 17
sorcery 4, 7
sound effects 21
special effects 16
spoon-bending trick 22, 23
stage 26
supernatural magic 20, 22

Topits 9
transforming tricks 24

vanishing tricks 12, 24

witchcraft 4, 8
word origins 4